SEASONS OF THE SPIRIT

SEASONS OF THE SPIRIT

Meditations of a Jogging Nun

Text By

The Sister Heléna Marie, CHS

Photographs by

Lorca Morello

ACKNOWLEDGMENTS

Grateful acknowledgment is extended to Sister Catherine Grace, for her encouragement, artistic advice and computer skills; to Sonja Hudson and James Armstrong, for their invaluable editing advice; and to all those at Morehouse Publishing who made sharing this work with others possible.

Morehouse Publishing
Editorial Office:
871 Ethan Allen Highway
Ridgefield, CT 06877

Corporate Office:
P.O. Box 1321
Harrisburg, PA 17105

Library of Congress Cataloging-in-Publication Data
Heléna Marie, Sister, C.H.S.
    Seasons of the spirit : meditations of a jogging nun/ text by Sister Heléna Marie, CHS : photographs by Lorca Morello.
        p.   cm.
    ISBN 0-8192-1571-6
    1. Meditations. 2. Christian life. I. Title.
BX2182.2.1145 1994: aa15 04-07-94
242' .802 — dc20
                                        94-15813
                                          CIP

Printed in Hong Kong

This book is for my Sisters, for their support, encouragement and tolerance; to all of the five-year-olds I taught during my eleven years at St. Hilda's and St. Hugh's School, and who taught me much about accepting the seasons of life as they come; and to Joshua and Jennie Rose, our convent hounds, who were not wildly enthusiastic about photo sessions, but who accompanied me faithfully and eagerly on many of my runs during the three years this book was in the making.

A WORD FROM THE PHOTOGRAPHER

I have known the Sisters of the Community of the Holy Spirit ever since I was a snow-suited toddler trudging daily along windy Riverside Drive to St. Hilda's and St. Hugh's, the school they ran on Manhattan's Upper West Side. When I returned for a visit many years later, the Reverend Mother introduced me to Sister Heléna Marie, who was just about to take her life vows. We felt as though we had always known each other, immediately discovering all sorts of common enthusiasms, from Eastern religions to drawing cartoons to running in the park as an indispensable relief from the confinements of city living.

By this time, St. Hilda's had expanded and moved out of the convent, and the Sisters, no longer solely a teaching Order, were seeking other means of livelihood, and I was one of the many New York artists desperately looking for space to work. Which is how I found myself living in what had once been my fourth grade classroom in the convent, and fixing up a piece of the old school lunchroom for my studio. Hoping to do a photo essay on the life of the Sisters, I was constantly lurking about with a camera, and it was from this that Sister Heléna Marie conceived the idea of having me take slides of the park that she would then use as the basis for a retreat. We embarked on a year of intensive picture taking, evolving through hundreds of pictures into a true collaboration of vision. We began to develop a language of seeing, a way of translating ideas into imagery and imagery into photographs that was simply understood between us. We encouraged each other through occasional doubts:

"But, Sister, it's *snowing!*"

"That's the best time for pictures!"

Or: "Maybe these pictures shouldn't have me in them."

"Yes, they should. Run up that hill again; I didn't get that last shot right."

Often we began with lists of pictures we wanted to take, but by the time we got to the places, we had seen so many interesting things along the way that we were nearly out of film. Working under severe budget constraints, we agonized over how to use the last couple of shots. Will that flower still be in bloom the next time we come out? Will that tree still have its leaves?

We always returned from these expeditions, sometimes frozen, usually late for something, but always tremendously exhilarated. I hope these pictures reflect the tremendous pleasure we had in taking them.

WARM UP

"A jogging nun?"

People often react this way when they see me running in New York City's Riverside Park. I usually grin and keep right on running. Yes, I am a Sister, and yes, I run, for to me jogging is a form of prayer.

Jogging anywhere, even on an indoor track or on the city streets, can induce a meditative state akin to prayer. But the park where I run is a place of special beauty which enhances this meditative state, corresponds to my inner struggles, and bridges the gap between the stillness of contemplation and the noise and bustle of the world — the *via contempliva* and the *via activa*.

At some point nearly every day I can be found running along what I call "my strip" — a narrow ribbon of greens and browns between Manhattan's Riverside Drive and the eastern bank of the Hudson River. Four miles long and at most an eighth of a mile wide, Riverside Park is only half a block from our convent. Over the years it has become for me a middle world between prayer and action.

Day after day I pound its turf, month after month throughout the year. The changing aspects of the park mirror what I experience in my life of prayer: periods of yearning, of pleading and agonizing, times of perseverance and determined patience, moments of desperation and panic, and bursts of wild praise and bubbling joy. This mirroring helps me to see myself more objectively and to connect my cloistered prayer with the rest of life all around me.

I invite you to travel with Lorca and me through a year of running. As you read my journal and look at her pictures, think of the runner as a symbol of the soul making its way through life, praying on the way; let Riverside Park stand for life. Seen this way, I am you, I am anyone. The image of the questing soul persists, page after page, the one constant amid the fluctuations of nature. Yet the soul also changes daily, seeing the same things each day with new eyes.

"But why do you run?" I am asked. I run because it makes me feel good, because it brings health and zest. I love to get my blood pounding rhythmically throughout my body, to fill my lungs to capacity. I run because it is a fantastically sensuous experience which thrills my eyes, ears, taste buds, skin. I run because I love to make contact with the earth and its plants and creatures, to feel the wind on my cheeks, to breathe the fragrances into my expanded lungs. I run to give expression to my sexual energy and to my creativity.

When I run, the effort I make, both physical and spiritual, unifies me and enables my whole organism to pray. I see God and his people at work in creation, and I pray for the world through which I run. My body itself forms a moving link between the inner and the outer. While limbs pump and the heart beats fast, the senses absorb a kaleidoscope of impressions and the spirit sings!

"Man is only an animal with a big brain," said the French mountaineer Maurice Herzog. "He makes such a fuss about the brain that he forgets arms, legs, pectoral muscles, as if he were ashamed of them." Jesus himself was a walker and an outdoorsman, preaching, healing, eating and sleeping outside, and walking hundreds of miles through the open countryside for the sake of the Kingdom.

IN, two, three, four; OUT, two, three, four; IN, two, three, four; OUT, two, three, four; IN . . . OUT . . . IN . . . OUT . . . .

Running is mostly a matter of getting enough air. When I first set out, my breathing is labored and self-conscious. My lungs stretch for air, my muscles crave the inflow of oxygen to the bloodstream. As I warm up, my lungs begin to feel nourished. My muscles relax and my breathing becomes gentle and rhythmic. After a while I am so attuned to my own breathing that I become centered. As the runner gasps for air, so, in prayer, we long for God. "As the deer longs for the waterbrooks, so longs my soul for you, O God."

My breathing, coordinated with my rhythmic footfalls, meshes with the breathing of life all around me. My heartbeat is synchronized with the heartbeat of the park, this world within and yet beyond the city. It coincides with the eternal rhythm of the universe, the diastolic/systolic pulse of life's seasons.

Between the vernal equinox and the summer solstice is a kind of inhalation. There is great plant activity; a period of quiet, steady growth follows, like a breath sustained and enjoyed. Then there is one more burst of activity between the autumnal equinox and the winter solstice, as the harvest moves into full swing — an exhalation, as fruit falls from the twig. Finally there is a period of quiet, the slumber of winter, a pause in the earth's breathing.

Seasons of the Spirit was originally created as a series of audio-visual meditations to be used as the basis for a three-day retreat. More than five hundred slides of the park were synchronized with music by Bach, Mozart, Messiaen and other classical composers. The stream of images and sounds, punctuated occasionally by short suggestive texts, was designed to encourage the retreatant to reflect on the seasons of her or his own life.

As a book, certain dimensions of this experience have necessarily been modified. Only a few select photographs have been used, and words are no substitute for music. But a book, because it leaves so much to the imagination of the reader, who can linger over the pages or turn them at will, involves its reader more creatively and more personally.

You don't have to be a jogger to identify with what follows. The experiences I have recorded are common to anyone who has prayed, meditated, quested or struggled. Come, journey with us through a year of running, and pray the seasons of your own life.

SUMMER STRETCH

Beep!
Wooooooossssshhh.
Honk, honk!
"Look out, Sister!"

Clad in an old faded habit and a pair of Nikes, I emerge from the trio of brownstones which form our convent, dash past the geranium-bedecked front stoop and down West 113th Street. I navigate the obstacle course of taxis, delivery boys and traffic islands on Riverside Drive. Preschool children call out with glee from playgrounds along the street; the sun shines on Jamaican nannies and curbside philosophers, ice cream vendors and German *au pairs*. The world is bright and boisterous.

I approach a graceful granite staircase. Twenty-one steps take me down, down from the sounds and activities of the street.

Suddenly I am in another world.

A retaining wall of native stone — Manhattan schist — drops dramatically to the park's floor. Magnificent rocks sparkle darkly, mica-flecked and sweating.

Like slipping from the city streets into a cathedral, I enter my park. Here it's immediately cooler. And green — all green! This is not the innocent baby-green of spring, but late August green, dangerous and *knowing*.

I breathe a sigh of relief, touch my toes in a reverent stretch and begin to run.

From every crevice ferns sprout, virulent, spider-like in their sinister delicacy. And power plants — poison ivy, stinging nettle, deadly nightshade — are at the most potent now.

Burdock stands shoulder-high in places, well-rooted by a juicy white tuber, thick and edible, which has thrust itself deeply into the earth. Its burrs, nature's velcro, clutch at clothing and skin. Two-foot leaves form a canopy of elephant ears over a bed of secrets — pillows of damp moss, underground ant colonies, rat families, perhaps even a homeless person seeking refuge from intruding eyes and glaring sun. Umbrella-like, the fuzzy leaves arch protectively, creating a mysterious shadow world.

What else does this dangerous green hold in its shade? A trembling rabbit, ever alert, listens for trouble. A Doberman Pincer, off her leash, sneaks like a panther, stealthy and sleek. Another jogger steps out of the shadows, light-footed, silent, gone.

Patches of plantain thrive in more open places. Its leaves, leathery and deeply veined, are sun traps, catching light and releasing oxygen to the jogger who is poised to run. Beaded seed stalks, drunk on sunlight, wave deliriously to neighboring clovers and green-fanged dandelion leaves.

Yellow-jackets buzz through the lace of light and dark, occasionally stopping to investigate a fallen blossom or a discarded tissue. In a different landing pattern, fluorescent flies touch down on crabgrass runways, translucent wings shimmering.

Overhead hangs a loft of broad leaves — catalpas, oaks, sycamores, maples, sweet gums (or liquid ambers, as they are called in my native California). From this balcony emerges a raucous counterpoint: squirrels' pizzicato, blue jays' brassy squawks, catbirds' glissando.

Beyond this choral clowning the park resonates like a fantasia of silky sounds, recalling the music of Debussy or Messiaen: layers of honey-sweet harmonies, sultry chords, complex multi-rhythms. I listen to wind sighing through the trees, bees droning from flower to flower, distant white noise, masquerading as breaking waves. I am mesmerized.

Slowly at first, then with increasing vigor I move through the woods; left, right, left, right, breathing in, out, in, out, . . . my breath and my footfalls praying in rhythm, "Thank you, God, for these last full days of summer." There is a fullness in prayer, too; times when one's yearnings in the spirit reach fulfillment and there is a knowing. These periods are gifts of the Holy Spirit,

given to us by God out of the outpouring of love for our strengthening and our joy. They are free and cannot be hoarded.

As I run, I pray,

"Bless this woodland, its plants and creatures."

"Bless my fellow joggers, bless the children playing, the watchful nannies."

"Bless the men and women who wander homeless through the park."

"Bless this summer world: luxurious beauty, danger, pain."

FALL DASH

When the first cool breezes blow down the Hudson, temperatures drop, the humidity vanishes and, suddenly, it's autumn. Excitement and electricity fill the air. Time now for beginnings: new programs get underway, a new school year opens, a new concert season begins. Behold, September!

Bach's fourth Brandenburg Concerto springs to mind, pulsing in time with my footsteps. Recorders and violins, violas and cellos encourage the surge of my blood.

I am inspired to make bold resolutions: "This year I'm going to run seven miles a day." "I'm going to follow a solid prayer schedule each day — two hours of meditation, an hour of Scripture reading, an hour's self-examination at night." "I won't make the same mistakes I did last year." "No laziness, no backsliding; *this* time I'm going to do it right!" I pound down the strip with renewed vigor.

But suddenly, a hot spell. A low ceiling of unmoving clouds traps smog. The heat drains me. The humidity is so thick I can hardly breathe. I don't feel like running; lethargy sets in. My wonderful prayer schedule collapses, and I feel like a failure. Dog days are back and I droop.

At times like these, when everything seems at a standstill, I find that it's important to do just that: stand still.

Stand still and listen to what God says to us in Scripture about our great plans and intentions: "Unless the Lord builds the house, your labor is in vain who build it."

Standing in the hot sun, I realize that my prayer schedule was my own project, something I was planning to accomplish under the power of my own steam and determination. But prayer isn't an accomplishment. It isn't self-devised, for it is God who prays in us, and the prayer is really God's.

I remember my original call to come to New York City and to become a member of the Community of the Holy Spirit. It was under these very trees that I responded to God's age-old question, "Whom shall I send?" "Here I am," I answered, "send me." Remembering this call and my response to it here among these elms (who, like sisters, seemed to encourage me), gives me the impetus to go on — not in my own strength this time, but in God's.

And so I get started again after a slack period, both praying and running, more aware this time that it is God who fuels both.

12

Mid-October finds me running through Indian Summer. Over my head the sun dances in a clear sky. Although the brightness of the sun keeps the stars and planets invisible, they are there, too — the same stars and planets that flickered their light upon the dinosaurs.

On a warm, smoky afternoon mystical light falls golden through trees. Southern-flying birds, having stopped in Riverside Park to bed and breakfast, linger songfully into the day. A formation of Canadian geese honks overhead, their one-way "V" pointing to winter shelter.

I stoop to examine the fallen leaves which have functioned so faithfully all season as laboratories for processing sunlight. Tired after a long career of photosynthesizing, the leaves have withdrawn their wild green lifeblood and are going out with one final blast of spectacular color.

First the elms, the lindens, and the horse chestnuts begin the ritual dance of color-turning; liquid ambers and maples join the organic fireworks display, then oaks and honey locusts. Sycamores reluctantly follow with a somber shift from green to brown, the lack of color-filled fanfare the price for their dawdling.

Poison ivy, still dangerous, sends crimson flames licking up tree trunks. The park's fruit-bearers swing into the harvest song; crabapples, cherries, rosehips and haw ripen together. Squirrels, preparing for winter, scurry through forests of goldenrod and purple asters to find acorns, walnuts, beechnuts, and peanuts tossed by a passerby.

I play hopscotch as I run along the path, leaping over a collage of autumn artifacts. The enormous fruits of the osage orange lie, like out-of-bounds tennis balls, here and there. Leaves from the ginkgo tree are discarded Oriental fans; the stinking fruit lies rotting, soft and sensual. Assorted seeds are mixed on the ground, desegregated: maple seed helicopters; spiky sweet gum pods; fuzzy sycamore balls; catalpa pods like long brown cigars, curling, crackling.

Life returns to the earth, its source, where it decays in her embrace. From this union comes death and the hope of new life, resurrection.

16

I run over the bones of the earth. Under me lies bedrock that is four hundred fifty million years old — in some places even a billion. I am a human being scampering over stone once trodden upon by dinosaurs, and before that, scoured by glaciers, and before that, covered by an ancient, primordial sea.

I am a temporary speck on the landscape. My whole life will be nothing more than a passing shadow on a rock structure which, although millions of years old, is itself only a transitory formation in a grander geological scheme.

As fall gets underway, I am mindful that it is a season of dying. In a shallow trough made in the bedrock by a glacier, I find some empty crack vials — a dimension of dying in a world now filled with reminders of death. Decaying leaves lie next to them, released by the wind from the once-verdant trees whose trunks will soon be mere skeletal reminders of the succulence of summer.

"Except a grain of wheat falls into the earth and dies, it remains alone; but if it dies, it bears much fruit." The dying leaves, too, speak of the central mystery of the Christian faith: dying to one's self so that new life in the spirit can arise. All the yellows, oranges, reds, and purples mix in a symphony of death. There is glory in this dying.

19

20

Finally the cold is here to stay. The temperatures have dropped from the nineties to the thirties; the excessive opulence of summer has faded, the harvest is complete and the long winter is poised a few degrees north — a day, a week ahead....

I put away my faded blue habits until next year. Along with my black habits, I pull out a substantial sweatshirt, a woolen cap and warm mittens.

On a late autumn evening we chant the First Vespers of Advent, and, with its theme of silence and anticipation, I prepare for winter.

WINTER MILES

The first snowfall! This morning I wake and, sensing the white hush, rise quickly. Our hounds, Joshua and Jennie, are ready.

Out of the warm convent we step into the icy dawn. Silence. Wonder! A surprise from the clouds has fallen during the night and we are the first to discover it in the morning light. New York stands white, in clean and delicate relief against a sky colored peach in the east and azure in the west.

The city lies sleeping, still and silent, under a blanket of snow crystals. Not a thing stirs, save for a lone bus at the end of the block, its rumbling muffled by the cold acoustical cushioning.

White. White! Everything is sparkling and clean, a picture of frozen softness: the trees, lampposts, parked cars and window ledges — everything is covered with a transforming layer of porous, magical snow.

The dogs strain at their leashes, noses quivering, dog tags jingling, tails beating like wild metronomes. Surrendering to their pull, I follow them down the front steps and past the snow-filled window boxes, their geraniums long ago moved to warmer quarters. Along the sidewalk we race, across the Drive, and down each snow-softened granite step to our place of worship and frolic. The park has become our winter playland.

I pause to examine a snowflake on my black sleeve. My morning meditation. Six sharp arrows point outward, protecting an exquisite web of frozen angles inside, a perfect geometric pattern, unique. I catch my breath at its beauty and send up a prayer of awe and gratitude. How did this delicate, perfect flake survive its long space journey from cloud to sleeve?

The dogs, impatient at this delay in their plans, are no longer able to restrain themselves, and dive into the powder. I, too, dance into the virgin snow and begin to jog.

We are making the first tracks of the day, blazing a trail which will be used by many others — cross-country skiers, joggers, winter-walkers — until the snow has been tromped upon and flattened into "the" path through the park.

Burdock skeletons jut brown and hollow from the snow bank, twigs and burrs dusted with white. The bulging black schist wall is speckled with hoarfrost. A soda can has metamorphosed into a miniature snow sculpture. Overhead, the leafless branches of the catalpas and oaks, maples and sweet gums are laden with fresh-fallen snow.

With every crunchy step our feet sink several inches, then squeak on the new-pressed snow. My socks are getting wet and my toes will soon be numb. In . . . out . . . in . . . out . . . My breath crystallizes in front of me on each "out."

Hallelujah! How I love being alive on this winter morning!

Winter is my favorite time to run. Running through the cold months of the year teaches me a lot about prayer. As there is the fun of playing in the snow, there is joy and playfulness in prayer. Thoreau once said, "I can see nothing so proper and holy as unrelaxed play in the bower God has built for us." Whether in bower or snow, play sometimes *is* prayer.

Running in winter involves overcoming obstacles, both outside of and within myself. Snow, ice, fierce winds off the river and below-zero temperatures become my opponents in this mock battle. Although it would be easier to stay inside, curled up under a cozy blanket, it's invigorating to wrap up in scarf, hat, and mittens, and to go out to meet the challenge. In prayer, too, there are times when it would be a lot easier and more enjoyable to read an extra chapter in my book than to go to chapel and pray. Putting on my running shoes and heading out into the cold influences me to pray when the time comes, just as praying regularly empowers me to run.

Miles later, our friskiness subdued, the dogs and I arrive back at the convent, now gently lit for Morning Prayer. I dry off the bright-eyed hounds, my ungloved fingers frozen stiff. (Will I be able to play the organ at morning Mass?)

The stairs creak as the Sisters make their way to the chapel. Each Sister, glimpsing the snow scene through the chapel windows, gasps in delight at the beauty, and I, rosy-cheeked and invigorated, smile.

There are other aspects of winter, too. When the snow melts, the park floor turns to mud and slush. I jog alone then, unwilling to drag the less discriminating dogs as I hop puddles and mudholes.

Then comes the next freeze. The puddles become miniature skating rinks, perfect for padded puppy paws. Icicles bolt down from rock overhangs like solid lightning streaks; mud hardens into ridges and ruts, castings of footprints and animal tracks.

Running after a winter freeze makes me mindful of the homeless people who dwell in the park. Smoke curls up through gratings from an abandoned subway station underneath the park. The homeless huddle against blazing subterranean trash cans, their only defense against the penetrating cold. I am fired to prayers of intercession.

"Lord, sometimes you had no place to lay your head. Watch over these brothers and sisters who must battle the ruthless winter without benefit of warmth and shelter."

The winter solstice arrives. December twenty-first is the shortest day of the year, and the longest night. The gradual lessening of daylight and increase of darkness can create a feeling of doubt and despair. We may feel oppressed, and wonder if this trend of increasing darkness will ever reverse itself. Or, will it continue, longer nights and shorter days, until darkness eclipses the light altogether?

We can reach a similar state in prayer. Like the winter landscape, our prayer seems lifeless and barren. A personal crises may have led to spiritual desolation, or perhaps our prayer has dried up and there seems to be no point in making any further effort. In the midst of such a state it is hard to be hopeful.

Yet, it is in the midst of winter, just four short days after the solstice, that we contemplate the birth of God to a young woman in Bethlehem. Christmas brings the hope that divine life can grow in us. Christ is born on one of the coldest, longest nights of the year.

January and February tick by; the park appears to be barren and lifeless, yet even now a closer look tells a different story. Red berries cling to bare branches. Multi-layered fungus steps boldly into view. Pigeons congregate around handfuls of bread crumbs scattered by a kind bird lover.

But by March the world is spent with cold and hunger, and so am I. By March mittens have been lost, linings in coats have begun to rip out, seams have split, and zippers are broken. We are tired of the cold and barrenness, and long for spring.

SPRING SPRINT

It all starts in the dark, oozing mud. Yet unsprung, the Paschal mystery lies in a rotting collection of decayed life-forms — dead leaves, seed pods, snail shells, centipedes and animal excrement — all mixed together, rained and snowed upon, crisscrossed by bicycle tracks, and stamped on by joggers.

What a great mystery: the mud of the earth is not only the place of death but also the very place of new life — resurrection. For in this mud the secret of life has lain, curled up in its little seed tombs.

Since September, when the seeds parachuted from trees and shrubs down to the soil, they have rested in the earth. They have waited through the spectacular autumn leaf show, through the first snows of winter, through the bitter cold of January and February. All the while the secret of life has been harbored in the dark and frozen mud.

Humus is a Latin word meaning "earth" or "ground." The word "humility" comes from the same root. Down in the humblest, lowest places the sacred mystery has been preparing itself. Life-potential gathers strength; unseen, leaf buds prepare for the burst of energy that will break open their tombs and send them yearning toward the sun.

And we have waited, too. Since the winter solstice, we have been waiting — for prayer to rekindle us, for the sun to heat up the days, for green and life and warmth and love. Each day the sun has risen a little earlier, set a little later, promising spring. My sisters and I sing a carol in chapel:

Tho' the cold grows stronger,

Yet the days grow longer,

Alleluia!

The countdown begins. We, too, wait with excitement and anticipation.

One day, without fanfare, like the gentle horn call that opens Brahms' First Piano Concerto, the first green shoots of spring rise from the earth — fragile spires of life. Green is rising out of the

dead brown; life is rising out of death. O blessed green, herald of the resurrection! Somehow more vigorous, our voices rise in song:

> Now the green blade riseth from the buried grain,
> Wheat that in dark earth many days has lain;
> Love lives again, that with the dead has been:
>> Love is come again,
>> Like wheat that springeth green.

Our hearts, too, respond to new life as we continue:

> When our hearts are wintry, grieving, or in pain,
> Thy touch can call us back to life again.
> Fields of our hearts that dead and bare have been;
>> Love is come again,
>> Like wheat that springeth green.

Although it is still cold, the days have been growing longer, slowly at first — only a minute every week. Soon light increases by a minute every other day. As the vernal equinox approaches, the sun rises earlier and earlier, sets later and later. The days get longer first by one minute, then by two. Day catches up with night, and when each is twelve hours long — the equinox — the battle has been won.

O victory! Each day some new variety of leaf uncurls from its bud. Succulent shoots burst from seed tombs. Chunks of chives pop up on the hillsides, and from every crack in a concrete city new life springs. A gentle green halo graces New York, a nimbus over a city of pain. Glory to God! The sap is rising, and green is coming back to the world!

And now — the colors! As inevitable as the circle of fifths, the flowers unfold in age-old sequence, as though connected by a giant world-timer. Between the shiny new blades of life,

their heads appear; first the crocuses, purple, yellow and white, then snowdrops and a few tulips. Our color-starved senses ache with an unaccustomed fullness.

A riot of color fills the landscape, and flowers of every hue and variety announce with the regal purity of trumpets and oboes their miraculous existence. Like musicians being signaled by the maestro, each flower and bud opens on cue in a symphony of petals, pistils, and leaves. Forsythia blush yellow and tender. Violets laugh through dry leaves, and Wordsworth's "host of golden daffodils" take the breath away.

Now nothing can stop the force of new life, which springs out of the old wounds, entwines unyielding metal and nudges concrete aside. All of nature shouts in a wild polyphony, from tulip to treetop, affirming gloriously the reality that in death there is life, the hope of resurrection.

When at last the pink cherries burst into bloom, the symphonic flower poem begins its full attack upon the senses. The great trees flower and, like goddesses adorned with pearls, display their splendor overhead. Horse chestnuts and black locusts drip with intoxicating fragrance. The heavy sweet perfume of the linden, overpowering and rich, makes me giddy. The orchid-like blooms of the catalpas climax this great biological fugue.

Every last, bitter moment of winter has been repented for, forgiven, and absolved with a blossom. Spring has outdone winter altogether, over compensating for the suffering, the cold, the desolation. The senses are drenched, and the soul exults in her Maker.

The mystery of spring has unfolded. Each day is warmer than the one before, and I change once more from winter black into summer blue. The park has come full cycle, and so have I, in praying as in running. At the height of spring, looking once more toward the fullness of summer, I am lifted to the highest form of prayer, the praise of our Creator.

Let the earth glorify the Lord....

Glorify the Lord, O mountains and hills,
and all that grows upon the earth....

Glorify the Lord, O springs of water, seas, and streams....

All birds of the air, glorify the Lord....

Glorify the Lord, O beasts of the wild....

O men and women everywhere, glorify the Lord....

From "A Song of Creation"
The Book of Common Prayer

38